SandCastle

Word Families Set 6

-ick as in kick

Pam Scheunemann

Consulting Editor Monica Marx, M.A./Reading Specialist

Published by SandCastle™, an imprint of ABDO Publishing Company, 4940 Viking Drive, Edina, Minnesota 55435.

Printed in the United States.

Credits
Edited by: Pam Price
Curriculum Coordinator: Nancy Tuminelly
Cover and Interior Design and Production: Mighty Media
Photo Credits: Brand X Pictures, Comstock, Digital Vision, Hemera, PhotoDisc, Stockbyte

Library of Congress Cataloging-in-Publication Data

Scheunemann, Pam, 1955-
     -Ick as in kick / Pam Scheunemann.
        p. cm. -- (Word families. Set VI)
     Summary: Introduces, in brief text and illustrations, the use of the letter combination "ick" in such words as "kick," "brick," "trick," and "wick."
     ISBN 1-59197-258-2
     1. Readers (Primary) [1. Vocabulary. 2. Reading.] I. Title.

PE1119 .S435154 2003
428.1--dc21

2002038220

SandCastle™ books are created by a professional team of educators, reading specialists, and content developers around five essential components that include phonemic awareness, phonics, vocabulary, text comprehension, and fluency. All books are written, reviewed, and leveled for guided reading, early intervention reading, and Accelerated Reader® programs and designed for use in shared, guided, and independent reading and writing activities to support a balanced approach to literacy instruction.

Let Us Know

After reading the book, SandCastle would like you to tell us your stories about reading. What is your favorite page? Was there something hard that you needed help with? Share the ups and downs of learning to read. We want to hear from you! To get posted on the ABDO Publishing Company Web site, send us e-mail at:

sandcastle@abdopub.com

SandCastle Level: Beginning

-ick Words

brick

chick

kick

pick

stick

wick

Sam put a heart on the brick wall.

Ann likes to pet the
chick.

Jo, Emma, and Meg
like to kick.

Mom had many flowers
to pick.

Eddy chose one stick.

Each candle has a
wick.

Slick and the Stick

Mia has a dog
named Slick.

One day Slick
went off
to chase a stick.

Slick came upon
a wall of brick.

15

16

Just that quick,
over went Slick!

On the other side,
Slick saw a chick.

18

Then Slick
watched a boy kick
a candle wick.

Slick went
through woods
that were very thick.

But Slick kept
on looking
until she
found the
stick!

The -ick Word Family

brick	quick
chick	sick
click	slick
flick	stick
kick	thick
lick	tick
pick	trick
prick	wick

Glossary

Some of the words in this list may have more than one meaning. The meaning listed here reflects the way the word is used in the book.

brick   a block of clay baked hard and used for building

chick   a young chicken or other young bird

pick   to gather by plucking or pulling

quick   very fast

wick   a twisted or woven cord used to draw fuel to the flame in a candle or oil lamp

About SandCastle™

A professional team of educators, reading specialists, and content developers created the SandCastle™ series to support young readers as they develop reading skills and strategies and increase their general knowledge. The SandCastle™ series has four levels that correspond to early literacy development in young children. The levels are provided to help teachers and parents select the appropriate books for young readers.

Emerging Readers
(no flags)

Beginning Readers
(1 flag)

Transitional Readers
(2 flags)

Fluent Readers
(3 flags)

These levels are meant only as a guide. All levels are subject to change.

ABDO
Publishing Company

To see a complete list of SandCastle™ books and other nonfiction titles from ABDO Publishing Company, visit **www.abdopub.com** or contact us at:

4940 Viking Drive, Edina, Minnesota 55435 • 1-800-800-1312 • fax: 1-952-831-1632